Indigo Gold
Poetry for the Soul

Down River Indigo

Indigo Gold Poetry for the Soul © 2024
Down River Indigo

All rights reserved.

No part of this publication may be
reproduced, stored in a retrieval system, or
transmitted, in any form or by any means,
electronic, mechanical, photocopying,
recording or otherwise, without the prior
written permission of the presenters.

Down River Indigo asserts the moral right
to be identified as the author of this work.

Presentation by *BookLeaf Publishing*

Web: www.bookleafpub.com

E-mail: info@bookleafpub.com

ISBN: 9789360941505

First edition 2024

To my dearest husband, moj muz, you are the sun that illuminates my sky and the moon that shines over my night. The wind in my sails pushing me across oceans and the stars guiding my way in the dark. Always embracing my tidal waves of emotion and uplifting my spirit, you have created the space for my soul to flourish and you have nourished every starved part of my heart. You encourage me everyday to follow my dreams and I am eternally grateful for you. I look forward every day to our beautiful life together. I am me, because of you. These words in this book would not be possible without your constant admiration and support. From the depths of my soul, thank you for being my person, my strength, my laughter and my eternal best friend. Volim te

For my boys, you two are my greatest accomplishments. You are the reason I live my life with as much passion and drive as possible. My endless life goal is to set an example for you to always follow your dreams and to give it your all. Life will have its mountains to climb and valleys to navigate. My only wish is that you both enjoy the view, smile along the way, and always look out for each other fiercely.

In loving memory of those I've lost in this lifetime...

To my Nico, your tenacity and determined spirit lives on forever in my heart. I'm reminded of your beautiful light with every breathtaking sunset you send my way. I know I'll see you on the other side. Give your dad a big hug for me.

Kirstin Ann, an angel even when you were earth side, you leave behind a legacy of pure love. For those you've encountered along the way, we are forever changed for the better because you existed in our lives.

To my mother, thank your for always guiding me in the right directions, even if it was away from you. I know you wished for life to have turned out differently, to be a positive part of your children's lives and a present mother, however your absence saved my life and has allowed generations of healing to occur within your bloodline. I see the struggles you endured and because of you I do my best to live my life in a better alignment. I acknowledge your hardships and recognize that if you did not fall on those swords, they could have been drawn for me. I hope you've found healing and peace in the afterlife. I've found solace knowing you are watching over and being there for us from the stars. Everytime I look up, I have faith you're looking down, and when I'm sitting under the glowing moon, that's when I can feel you're here.

ACKNOWLEDGEMENT

To my dad, thank you for raising wild children with free spirits and determined souls. Teaching us as young children to adapt to any situation and overcome any obstacle, you've successfully passed down your knowledge of hunting, fishing and living outdoors creating infinite memories and experiences along the way. You have created the environment for me to thrive in nature and be fearless in the face of anything. Your sacrifice through the years does not go unnoticed.

Granny, thank you for always being a strong and independent role model, being a display of grace and poise. You were a huge component of introducing nature into our lives, always bringing us to the dam, fishing with us and having us watch nature documentaries. This entire book was written while staying with you on the water next to the bay. I'll never forget the laughs, the conversation and the companionship. Nana, thank you for prioritizing water in our lives. Taking the time to teach us to swim as tiny babies was the foundation for our abilities under the waves. You are the matriarch of a family of mermaids.

Jen (She's a God, Podcast), thank you for giving me the confidence to use my voice and to tell my story. You have catapulted me into this experience of sharing my journey of heartbreak and healing. I am grateful to have crossed paths with you in this lifetime.

PREFACE

Indigo is a plant that gives us beautifully colored dyes that are a deep blue similar to the colors that radiate from the depths of the oceans. The ocean is a place I am deeply connected to. My dearest childhood memories consist of exploring reefs, tide pools, and free diving with the creatures fearlessly. It has always been and will always be a place that I feel the most at home. Where I am wrapped in the embrace of my Mother. It is our original womb. Where all life has been created and nourished.

The name "Indigo child" is capable of being adopted by almost anyone who has a deep connection to the Earth. It has commonly been used to describe a child that has been brought up in nature and consequently has a heightened awareness and resonating connection to the elements, the plants and the animals. A word that could perfectly describe my siblings and I.

I grew up right on the banks of the Root River in Wisconsin. As children, my siblings and I were baptized by the muddy waters of the River. I learned to swim with the current and against it. I connected with the creatures that inhabited it. We feasted from the abundance it provided. I learned to create and control fire along its banks. Almost daily we would drift, swim or paddle up and down the river. As children we respected its power and its unpredictability. We adventured around enough to know that shortly down the river, the water was always slow. We knew there would be shallow waters where you could stand and catch your breath. Along the banks, you can grab hold of the vegetation and tree roots and climb out of it for a rest. My confidence and connection with the water made me very capable in my everyday life. Making it simple to acknowledge that life flows and comes and goes just like our river. It can be navigated in similar ways as well. Sometimes the current is strong and if you can swim with it and respect it, it will take you far and fast. Sometimes it is slow and if you drift quietly enough a painted turtle might just mistake you for a log and climb right on for a nap in the sun. There may be rocks lining the bottom you run into along the way. Huge logs and debris blocking waterways. Maybe the most significant similarity could be that the water in the river always flows down and onward. Eventually leading out to the beautiful oceans. It continues its way regardless of what is in its path. Despite whatever happens in life or in the river, if you flow with it, eventually it will lead you to calm waters.

As a child I was intuitively drawn to listening to the sounds around me. I always remembered to take a moment to listen to the birds. Their songs always serve as a lullaby to calm the mind. Our nervous systems have learned to rely on the birds' songs as being confirmation of being in a safe location.

While I was serving in the Marine Corps, I was fortunate to be stationed on the very small island of Okinawa. What they lacked in miles they made up for in the natural and picturesque land they cared for. Rare was it to see trash or debris littering the streets, beaches or waterways. Their culture was one of understanding their connection to the Earth, and how to live symbiotically. The warm turquoise waters were life changing and the vast sky illuminated my mind. I will never forget all of the time spent in the water connecting with the creatures and the land. They have a beautiful way of mending broken pottery back together when it has been cracked or shattered. They fuse the pieces back together very delicately with a material that is a breathtaking gold. It is a mindful way of reminding us that even when we are broken, those exact cracks are what make us beautiful, unique and valuable. It takes a lot of time to mend these pieces. Sometimes the same piece will need to be repaired many times. As the pottery breaks more and more and needs to be mended, it eventually becomes a stronger piece of pottery. Unique in all of its golden cracks. Similar to all of us experiencing the traumas and joys of living this beautiful life we've been gifted. Embrace your golden cracks and all of the experiences that come with them.

My entire life, I was constantly battling between wanting to open up and express my emotions while simultaneously shutting them down and shoving them back down into the eternal dark abyss that was the feeling in my soul. Always afraid to speak my mind and share my true emotions for fear of being compared to my mother. Tip toeing around my true reality never letting anyone glimpse at the pain running through my veins. That is until I took pencil to paper and started to write it all down. Like a tidal wave or avalanche the words came flowing out of me in beautiful harmony not only healing so many internal wounds that lived beside them but helping others along the way. I hope these words bring you healing, growth and the inspiration to keep going on this magnificent journey we call life.

Generational Trauma

So many pairs of humans
hidden within our souls

The trauma inherited from our ancestors
it weighs heavy and takes a toll

Generational and familial pain
always finding ways of trickling down

Addiction, anger, sadness and shame
emotions so strong you're sure you'll drown

Some mothers cannot mother their children
they've been deemed "unfit" or "unsound"
but what happens to the children
when their mothers are not around?

Blood Brothers

There's nothing like having a brother
and growing up side by side

They are the only ones who could understand
the only ones whose lives with yours coincide

You don't have to explain your life story
or details of your past

When you are together
there's comfort, reminiscing and laughs

A feeling of ease and safety
is always found with them close by

Don't take this time for granted
things change in the blink of an eye

Moon Mentality

The moon had a way
of amplifying her pain

Turns out she wasn't crazy
and the moon affects her brain

She has the ocean in her veins
holding onto emotions like waves

Rising and falling with the tides
two different personalities collide

A beautiful cobra spitting venom
striking with spiteful words

Under the glow of the moon
like a werewolf she turns

From a loving and concerned mother
to a dragon that burns

Motherless Daughter

Like a black cat in the night
she came and went in a flash

I was anticipating the inevitable
and waiting for the crash

I still remember the agony
of crying to sleep at night

Wishing for her to come home
and holding my blanket tight

I still remember the feeling
of the chill upon my cheeks

The tears staining my pillow
and the pillow masking shrieks

I was a motherless daughter
navigating these waters without her

I thought my emotions were strong
but I bet hers really gnawed her

I have no idea what it's like

being a mother without your daughter

I don't even know what's worse
all I know is I applaud her

Oceans in Me

The ocean resides
inside of me
the iron in my blood
is the same as the seas

Crashing and rolling
so effortlessly
ebbing and streaming
flowing so free

It can't be contained
or locked up and chained
it's free to rise
and fall unconstrained

My emotions are the tides
the highs and lows can decide
how I will feel
on the inside

I can be a tsunami or a wave
sustain life or become a grave

in the darkest of my depths
is where the weak become brave

Motherless Motherhood

Becoming a mother without one
it's an unexplainable feeling

It's simultaneous heartbreak
and your ultimate healing

You're baptized by the pain
to the realm of motherhood

The things that used to be unclear
are suddenly and sadly understood

An overwhelming love
fixes up your broken cracks

You momentarily realize
how much a mother's love impacts

I used to question why she left
how could a mother abandon her own kin?

Then I realized
how powerful her demons were
and saw that it was a war she wouldn't win

I watched her fall upon her swords
And because of her I would not fight

The battle against the bottle
She saved me in hindsight

10

Working Mama

The first day that I had to leave you
my heart was ripped right from my chest

I don't know why
everyone tried to validate it
and tell me that it was for the best

You were a tiny little baby
so fragile and brand new

Now my only memories of younger you
are the clothes that you outgrew

I signed my name on the dotted line
and according to the military
a son wasn't assigned

They didn't care about the bond
or the well-being of the mother
To them it was perfectly okay
for the child to be raised by another

Long days
and even longer nights

So many different homes
and long distance flights

The best thing that could have happened
was my military career coming to an end

That's when my life truly started
with you this time I'd like to spend

12

Death of a Brother

Together we thought
we could conquer anything

Invincible, indestructible
always jumping higher off the swings

Running, climbing, swimming and play
who knew that it would be gone one day

We lost you before
the flowers bloomed that May

April's showers came down heavy
and our skies were always gray

Now you're a willow tree
and a stone carved name
and since that day
nothing's been the same

Every year I visit you
during the fireworks of July

I'm always there with you
watching under the same sky

Grief

Grief is a dark shadow
continually following you around

Like the shell of a human
everywhere you look it is found

It's often showing up
with even the smallest amount of light

And on the brightest and sunniest days
it seems to be the darkest that same night

An abyss
a black hole
a siphon of light

Stealing the breath
and making a chest that is tight

Nightmares and memories
keeping you awake

Like trying to learn how to swim
at the bottom of a lake

Everyone grieves
at their very own pace

The best thing you can do
is give a grieving soul grace

When We Go

No matter the time
the person or the place
he was always ready to give
a big smile and embrace

In a room full of people
he'd be the first to stand
make eye contact with you
and firmly shake your hand

He was thoughtful and kind
constantly reminding others
they were always on his mind

His laughter could cure
the cloudy and rainy days
No matter the time or place
he always had a witty phrase

Even when we know
we won't be having all the time

There's never enough memories
and losing you feels like a crime

I like to think that your happy now

and healthy as can be

Running, playing, riding and singing
and that your soul is finally free

My Sun

I never believed in a god
until he came around

Lighting up my universe
sprouting life from barren ground

Like the stillness found
after every exhale

He calmed my storms
without any fail

His presence was nourishing
his touch a tonic

He can make me laugh harder
than any great comic

I never believed in a god
until he came around

providing joy in abundance
eradicating frowns

listening close to every word I'd say
when life got hard
he would always stay

He puts me on a pedestal
reminding me of my worth

He always makes me feel
like I'm the luckiest girl on earth

You see
there has to be a God
who sent him straight to me

The universe aligned
he's part divine
because of him

I believe

Mother from Another

She was gifted from the heavens
handpicked from God himself

Like an angel in an apron
she should be honored on a shelf

Life has given her many struggles
She even knows her way around a knife

I would travel to the ends of the earth for her
I would even trade my life

She came to me by marriage
becoming the mother I never had

She created and raised my favorite human
because of her I'm eternally glad

Sister across the Sea

My dearest and beloved sister
your beautiful heart is deeply missed

Our souls are parted by the seas
but I'm so delighted that you exist

I love your brother immensely
he's truly been god's greatest gift

Thank you for sharing his heart with me
because of you we are never adrift

The most genuine human being
you deserve the whole world and even more

We will always find our way back to you
the way the waves always meet the shore

Moon Magic

Most of the days
I don't need to look outside

I can feel that you are here
your pull creating a tide

Tidal waves initiated
the moons power creates shifts

Channeling divinity
and activating gifts

Let go and release
imagine, visualize, and manifest

Send negative talk away
and let self doubt take a rest

Death before Reunion

Miles and miles between us
thousands of words left unsaid
we always think we'll have more time
but your born

you blink

and you're dead

All along it was pointless
to be angry, resentful and bitter
holding expectations over her head
because we never considered

How quickly anger turns to sadness
when death is delivered

Anger to Acceptance

I used to be so angry
rage welling up inside

Until the day you left us for good
and I found out you finally died

I thought about this moment
for eternity it seems

I never thought it would hit me this hard
that I'll only see you in my dreams

I spent a lot of time
forgiving your mistakes
now the hole you left in my heart
is healed but it still aches

I'm so grateful that I've found
space in my heart to forgive you

I only wish before you died
I told you and you knew

Dream of Greed

How can a human walk into a forest
And his first dream is of greed?

The oaks try to reason with him
but he doesn't talk to the trees

When the axes are swung
he doesn't hear their pleas

Leaving stumps to bleed
he takes corpses and leaves

Artificially fertilized
and plants poisonous seed

Pockets to be lined
with more than they need

He mislabels medicine
calling it a "weed"

Hiding the magic of the dandelions
to intentionally mislead

We consume modified veggies
and our meat is eating "feed"

Monoculture and pesticides
will surely kill the bees

Earth Healing

Dearest Mother Earth
How can I thank you for your healing?

You've helped me rid myself of doubt
released the trauma I was concealing

Your sunshine is my medicine
your ocean my oasis

Combine the two and add clear skies
a perfect recipe for homeostasis

Your mountains fresh crisp air
your diversity of existence

I'm constantly in awe of your beauty
as I travel along your distance

Nature Intended

Natural birth was an odyssey
an accomplishment I strongly desired

It was my journey to birth sovereignty
A badge of honor I finally acquired

I had done it at last
9 months of dedication and commitment

The pain was transformative
and worth the fulfillment

With a thunderous roar
he arrived safe and sound

I was on top of the world
sitting on a throne with a crown

Emotionally aware
grounded, connected, and divine
purely amazed, physically unfazed
in awe of God's perfect design

Nectar of Life

In the act of feeding a child
there is a certain magic that can be found

In the breast of a new mother
you'll find something quite profound

When the babies saliva meets
like a computer it reads

Nature then creates the best formula
knowing exactly what baby's body needs

Blissful and content
drifting off to sleep

It's a sacred and cherished bond
one that can not ever be beat

A concoction of happiness
floods the mama's brain

Creating a thriving baby
and a mother just the same

Eternal Gratitude

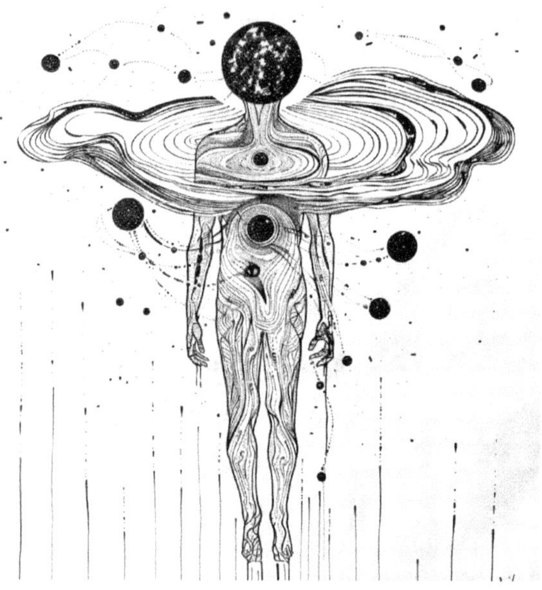

I wish I could scream it from the rooftops
for all the world to hear

"You're a divine and powerful being!"

"Stop living your life in fear!"

We are programmed to believe
the world is a terrifying place

But if you travel
you will determine
that is is not at all the case

The world is filled with wonder
beauty, divinity, and grace

You can witness the nature of humanity
with every smiling face

Don't get caught up with the news
or get wrapped up in the sadness

Think ahead
make sure books are read
and don't contribute to the madness

A Strong Vessel

Strive to be
as patient as the trees
and more powerful
than the highest of seas

You only get one physical home
this body your soul was given
take care and love your earth-side vessel
and keep your muscles in good condition

Let movement be your medicine
and breath be your escape
eat food that grows up from the ground
and don't focus on your shape

Kintsukuroi

The vase fell and shattered
broken beyond repair
until the day
the potter came this way
and fixed it up with care

He filled in all the cracks
with a brilliant and glistening gold
now something that used to be broken
is a beautiful art piece to behold

The same should be said
about a human's broken heart

Those who survive heartbreak
are stronger than the start

Fill in your broken cracks
with care and a sparkling gold
display all of your scars
shimmer like the stars
let your unique beauty truly unfold

Sunshine Mind

Plant a garden inside your soul
and water it with self-love
be the sunshine that gives it life
and send nourishment from above

Dig your hands into your dirt
rip up your unwanted roots
prune your trees
find strength in the breeze
soon you'll be creating fruits

Our Home Country

My home country isn't here
it's somewhere else
between near and unclear

I've traveled so far
found and lost people a plenty
I've discovered since then
most alliances are empty

Longing for belonging
in a place I don't belong
I force and fight
and try to make right
something that is so wrong

This place that I see
is supposed to be
home of the brave
and the land of the free

We somehow forgot
about the founding people and the tea
now all the neighbors seem to do
is stay divided and disagree

No-one is standing together
we've all dropped down to our knees

I hope one day
our children will change the world and say
we heard our parents' pleas

Animal Teachers

I'll never forget my animal teachers
I keep meeting along the way

The creatures crossing my life path
all have an important message to convey

When the birds tell me to soar
it may be obvious it seems

but they don't imply
to actually 'fly'
they're talking about my dreams

They beg me to jump
dare me to be fearless on the edge
teaching me faith in my own wings
as they fly beside me off the ledge

Two Birds

I saw two cardinals
playing in the wind
instantly I knew it was you

Coming to visit me
on this overcast day
you help me make it through

Even without your physical presence
you both find ways to warm my heart

I cherish the sunsets
and birds that you've sent me
all these days we've been apart

Climb a Tree

Let your bare feet
connect to the bark

The strength of the wind
will help fuel your spark

Wrap two hands around branches
feel the warmth of the sun

Your heart will start to heal
when you stop trying to outrun

Our true nature is to climb
always seeking a beautiful view

So find a tree
I guarantee
Your soul knows what to do

Down the River

Off I go to another world
I hope you come along

Down the River with the Indigo
where we are immersed in Nature's song

Let's share in the medicine
amongst the plants that make us strong

explore outside and let Nature show you
you're in the right place
and you belong

War Wound or Women

The earth demands a sacrifice
by war wound
or by women

We can slaughter each other
or use our intuition

There is a reason only women
are capable of birth

From the beginning
we are tasked
to facilitate earth's rebirth

torn in half
delivering a soul
yet our body remains unhurt

By being outside and sitting still
we can bleed into the dirt

Without a wound
we can release
the negativity of the earth

Moms without Mothers

No sick days or vacations
No "proud of yous" or "great jobs"

I'm used to having no expectations
but part of me feels robbed

I wish my mom could hold me
brush my hair back when I'm ill

Moms without mothers
are good at taking care of others
They're always holding it together until...

Stress becomes a wildfire
burning us alive

We beg, we plead
we pray and wish
our moms were there to help us survive

Instead of given a teaching
we were part of the lesson

Now we are wholeheartedly there for our kids
stopping the parental absence procession

Dive into the Depths

You are allowed to be
a mountain and a tree

The mountain is unmoving
and extends into the sky
the trees live to sway in the breeze

One is a haven for the birds that fly high
and the other is a home for the bees

We are all made from the sun and stars
80% ocean and our ancestors' scars

We have tides within us rising and falling
Dive into your depths
Discovery is calling

Connected

Magic always flows
like effortless waves in the sea

The earth greets my feet
like the flower meets the bee

When I walk into a forest
the forest echoes in me

I witness my fingerprints
in every ring of a tree

It's where I go as "Me"
And leave as a "We"

It's where I always run to
the place I feel most free

www.ingramcontent.com/pod-product-compliance
Lightning Source LLC
LaVergne TN
LVHW021242200726
843509LV00012B/1573